VIOLIN SCALE BOOK FOR BEGINNERS

HARRY HUNT, JR., MFA

Violin Scale Book for Beginners

Published by Harry Hunt, Jr.
Chicago, IL
harryhuntjr.com

ISBN: 978-1-954127-13-5 (Paperback)

Printed in the USA
First Edition

CONTENTS

PLAY-ALONG PRACTICE TRACKS

To Stream or Download Click or Visit harryhuntjr.net/book-vsbfb

OTHER LINKS:

Stream from Bandcamp
https://vsbfb.bandcamp.com/releases

Download from Dropbox
https://bit.ly/violinscalebfb

(bookmark links in your browser for quicker access)

INTRODUCTION

Are ready to learn your first violin scales?

This book contains easy one-octave scales and exercises in first position.

Each scale contains an easy-to-read fingerboard diagram for each scale. There are scale variations in quarter-note, eighth-note, and slurred patterns.

Learning scales helps to build your tone and finger patterns in different keys.

There are practice drone tracks provided in each key to help with your practice. Drones can be a great help with intonation.

A MAJOR SCALE (High)

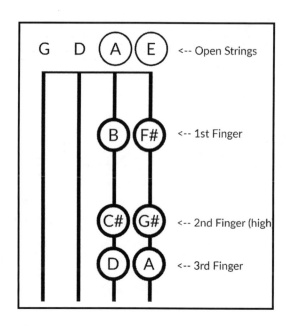

FINGERING

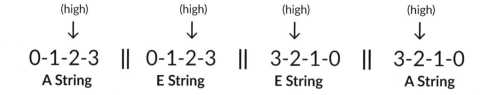

(high)		(high)		(high)		(high)
0-1-2-3	‖	0-1-2-3	‖	3-2-1-0	‖	3-2-1-0
A String		E String		E String		A String

NOTATION

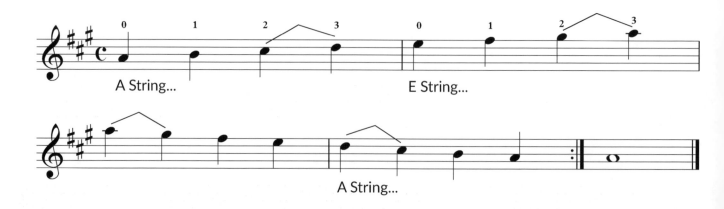

A MAJOR SCALE (Quarter Patterns)

A MAJOR SCALE (8th Patterns)

A MAJOR SCALE (Slur Patterns)

G MAJOR SCALE (Low)

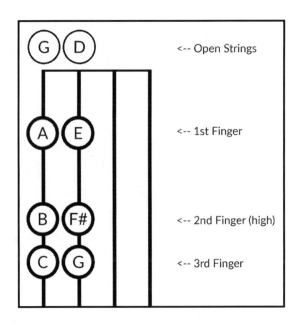

FINGERING

NOTATION

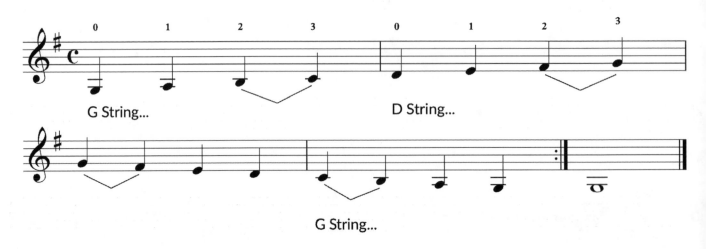

G MAJOR SCALE (Quarter Patterns)

G MAJOR SCALE (8th Patterns)

G MAJOR SCALE (Slur Patterns)

1

2

3

4

5

D MAJOR SCALE

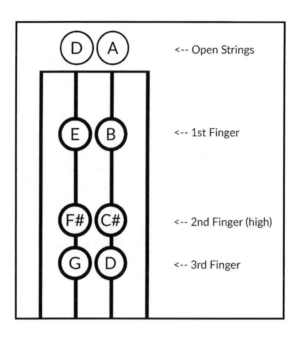

FINGERING

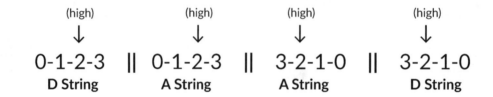

(high)	(high)	(high)	(high)
↓	↓	↓	↓
0-1-2-3 ‖	0-1-2-3 ‖	3-2-1-0 ‖	3-2-1-0
D String	A String	A String	D String

NOTATION

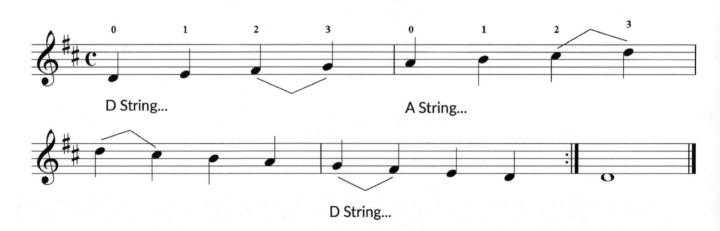

D String...

A String...

D String...

D MAJOR SCALE (Quarter Patterns)

D MAJOR SCALE (8th Patterns)

D MAJOR SCALE (Slur Patterns)

1

2

3

4

5

C MAJOR SCALE

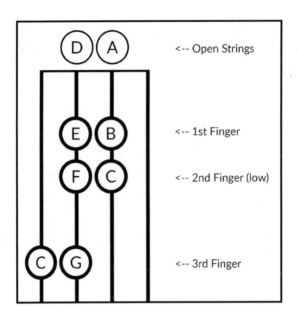

FINGERING

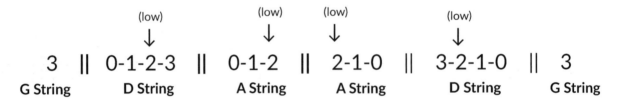

NOTATION

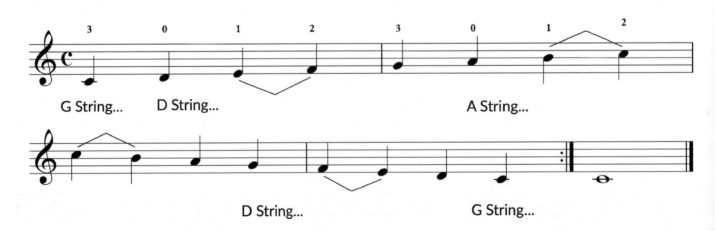

©2021 Harry Hunt, Jr.

C MAJOR SCALE (Quarter Patterns)

C MAJOR SCALE (8th Patterns)

C MAJOR SCALE (Slur Patterns)

A MAJOR SCALE (Low)

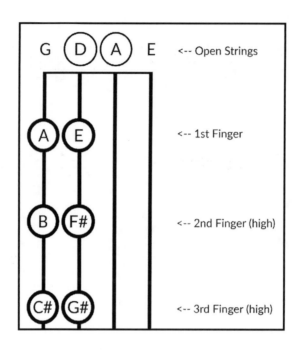

FINGERING

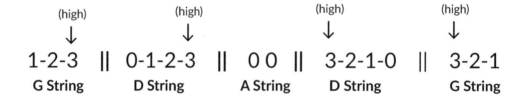

(high)	(high)	(high)	(high)
↓	↓	↓	↓
1-2-3 ‖	0-1-2-3 ‖	0 0 ‖	3-2-1-0 ‖ 3-2-1
G String	D String	A String	D String G String

NOTATION

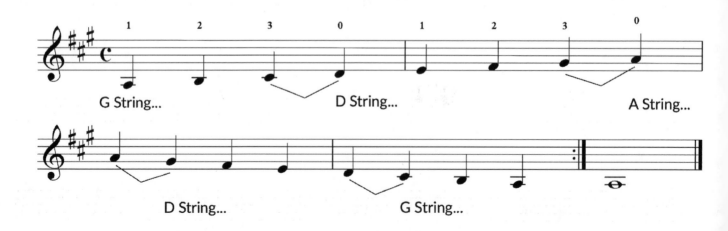

G String...   D String...   A String...

D String...   G String...

A MAJOR SCALE (Quarter Patterns)

A MAJOR SCALE (8th Patterns)

©2021 Harry Hunt, Jr.

A MAJOR SCALE (Slur Patterns)

1

2

3

4

5

F MAJOR SCALE

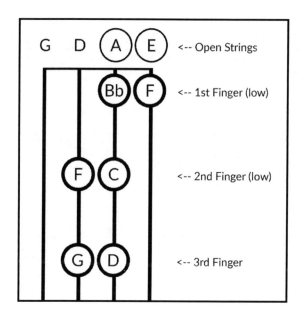

FINGERING

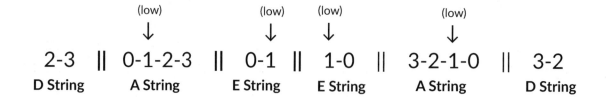

NOTATION

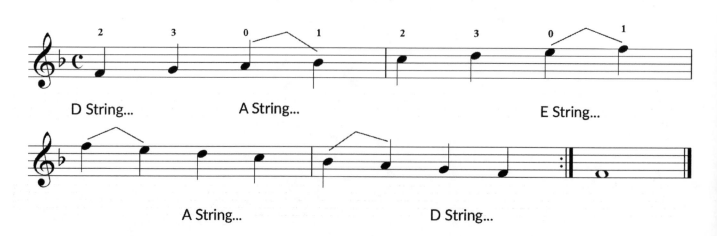

©2021 Harry Hunt, Jr.

F MAJOR SCALE (Quarter Patterns)

F MAJOR SCALE (8th Patterns)

F MAJOR SCALE (Slur Patterns)

1

2

3

4

5

G MAJOR SCALE (High)

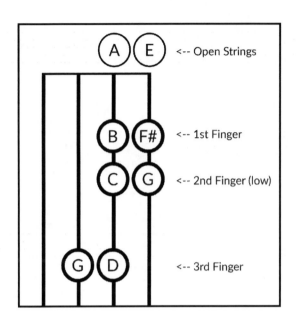

FINGERING

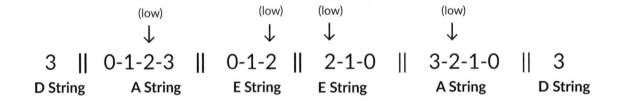

NOTATION

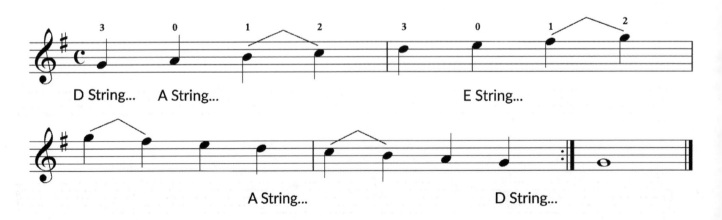

G MAJOR SCALE (Quarter Patterns)

G MAJOR SCALE (8th Patterns)

G MAJOR SCALE (Slur Patterns)

33

Bb MAJOR SCALE

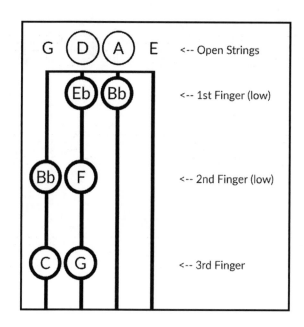

FINGERING

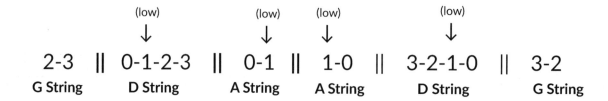

(low)	(low)	(low)	(low)
2-3 ‖ 0-1-2-3 ‖ 0-1 ‖ 1-0 ‖ 3-2-1-0 ‖ 3-2			
G String D String A String A String D String G String			

NOTATION

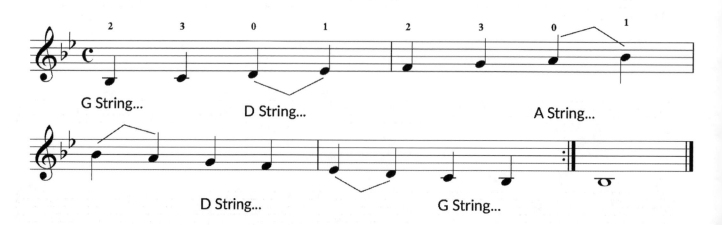

©2021 Harry Hunt, Jr.

Bb MAJOR SCALE (Quarter Patterns)

Bb MAJOR SCALE (8th Patterns)

Bb MAJOR SCALE (Slur Patterns)

24 EASY CLASSICAL VIOLIN SOLOS: BOOK 1

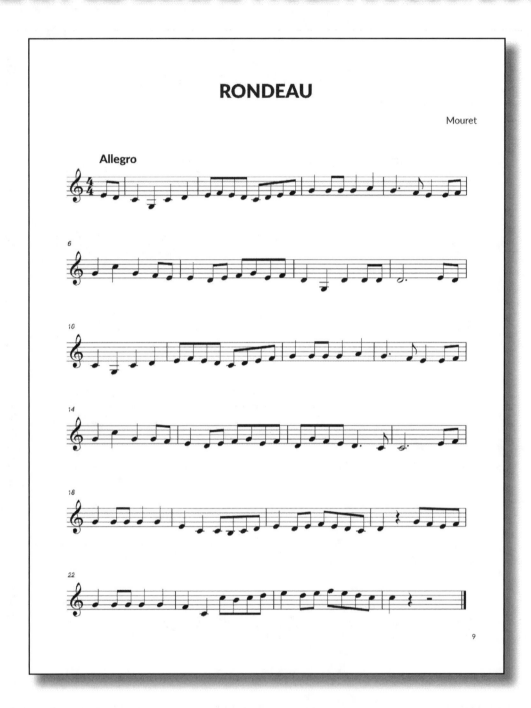

24 Easy Classical Violin Solos has short and simple pieces of some of your favorite classical melodies.

The music comes from classical composers such as: *Bach, Mozart, Beethoven, Haydn, Handel, Brahms and more.*

harryhuntjr.com/violin-bookstore

CLASSICAL HITS FOR JAZZ VIOLIN

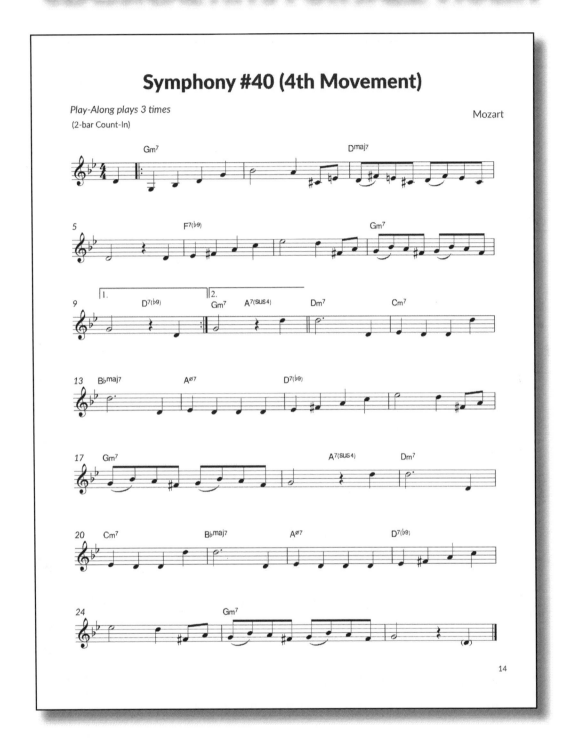

Play your favorite classical melodies along with jazz play-along backing tracks.

Classical Melodies for Jazz Violin does not require any improvisation. You can just have fun, read the melodies and play along with the jazz audio track.

harryhuntjr.com/violin-bookstore

24 EASY CLASSICAL VIOLIN SOLOS: BOOK 2

24 Easy Classical Violin Solos has short and simple pieces of some of your favorite classical melodies.

The music comes from classical composers such as: *Bach, Mozart, Beethoven, Mendelssohn, Vivaldi, Tchaikovsky and more.*

harryhuntjr.com/violin-bookstore

Made in the USA
Columbia, SC
28 January 2024

31068234R00024